ENTERTAINMENT'S

TOP 10

TECHNOLOGY TOP TENS

SANDY DONOVAN

Lerner Publications Company • Minneapolis

Lerner Publications Company
A division of Lerner Publishing Group, Inc.
241 First Avenue North
Minneapolis, MN 55401 USA

For reading levels and more information, look up this title at www.lernerbooks.com.

Library of Congress Cataloging-in-Publication Data

Donovan, Sandra, 1967–
    Technology top tens / by Sandy Donovan.
        pages   cm. — (Entertainment's top 10)
    Includes index.
    ISBN 978–1–4677–3841–5 (lib. bdg. : alk. paper)
    ISBN 978–1–4677–4677–9 (eBook)
        1. Video games—Juvenile literature. 2. Video games industry—Juvenile literature.
    3. Application software—Juvenile literature. 4. Blogs—Juvenile literature. I. Title.
    GV1469.3.D667 2015

Where would we be without technology? It lets you play games, chat with friends, move from place to place, and answer burning questions with a few keystrokes. Technology is all around us—in our gadgets, in our vehicles, and in new inventions big and small.

But do you ever think about what makes a particular piece of technology the very best of its kind? Or wonder about the companies and workers behind those products?

We do! And we've sorted through facts and stats to figure out just what the best are. Check out our top 10 lists of tech standouts, from the most popular smartphone apps to the highest-paying tech careers. We've used hard data such as website views, sales numbers, and average salaries to rank our items. Ready to take a look at technology's trendsetters and trailblazers? Turn the page and plunge in!

The Wii *(below)* and Nintendo DS are just two of the video game consoles that Nintendo has produced over the last 40 years. Is this company the No. 1 video game maker? Read on to find out!

The 1970s just called. They're wondering about these things called video games. Are they any good? Will they catch on at all? You know the answer. In just a few decades, video game making has gone from a brand-new idea to a multibillion-dollar industry. Below we've ranked the top game makers according to the latest yearly profits reported by each company.

10. Capcom: $952 million

What do *Mega Man, Monster Hunter, Resident Evil,* and *Street Fighter* have in common? They were all made by this Japanese gaming firm. Capcom has been going strong since it started putting out coin-operated games such as *Little League* in 1983. In fact, Capcom is short for Capsule Computers, the term originally used to describe those early '80s arcade games.

<<<< **9. Konami: $1.2 billion**

This Japanese company is responsible for hit games including *Dance Dance Revolution, Castlevania,* and *Yu-Gi-Oh!* It first launched in 1983 as a jukebox rental company, and then it branched out into video games, toys, trading cards, special effects films, and more. (The $1.2 billion earnings that landed it on this list are for just the video game department.)

Dance Dance Revolution involves a floor pad where players step on arrows in sequence with a character on-screen. The game started as an arcade game before expanding into a play-at-home version.

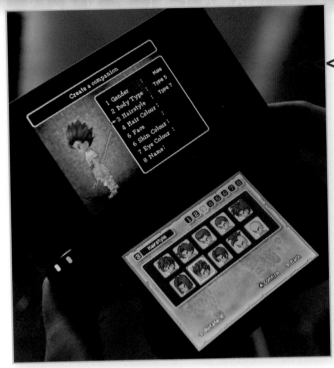

<8. Square Enix: $1.4 billion

What happens when a video game company called Square merges with one called Enix? We get a new company called Square Enix, of course! Since that 1983 merger, this Japanese company has been best known for its role-playing video game series, including the *Final Fantasy* series, the *Dragon Quest* series *(left)*, and the *Kingdom Hearts* series.

7. Ubisoft: $1.62 billion

This French company started out as a computer game publisher in 1986. It was founded by five brothers in a small rural town. These days it has 29 studios in 19 countries. It's best known for *Assassin's Creed, Far Cry,* and *Rayman*. In 2011, Ubisoft created its own film division with plans to produce shows and films based on its games.

6. Sega: $3.33 billion

Sega got its start in Hawaii in 1940, when it was known as Service Games. In the 1950s, its American owners moved it to Japan and started making coin-operated arcade games. But the company took off in the 1980s as one of the world's largest home video game console makers. It's currently making money from games such as *Super Monkey Ball Touch & Roll* for the Nintendo DS and *Football Manager* for the Xbox 360.

5. Electronic Arts: $4.14 billion

This California-based video game developer has been around since 1982. Its vast collection of titles includes sports series such as *Madden NFL, FIFA,* and *NBA Live* as well as adventure games such as *Battlefield, Need for Speed,* and *Medal of Honor.* And don't forget *The Sims,* the super-popular series of strategy-based virtual world games. Electronic Arts also partners with LucasArts to make *Star Wars: Knights of the Old Republic.*

4. Activision Blizzard: $4.85 billion

Another combination company, this one came from the 2008 merger between Activision and Blizzard Entertainment. Although it's now one business, the California company still puts out games under two labels. Activision has produced the hit series *Call of Duty, Skylanders,* and *Guitar Hero.* Meanwhile, Blizzard Entertainment is responsible for the *Warcraft, StarCraft,* and *Diablo* series.

Instead of a traditional game controller, Guitar Hero uses a guitar-shaped controller to operate the menu screens and game play.

3. Nintendo: $6.47 billion

This Japanese company has been around for more than 130 years! In the 1880s, it manufactured playing cards. By the 1970s, Nintendo was making home video game consoles. The big break came with *Donkey Kong* in 1981. More recently, Nintendo has been best known for its handheld devices: 1989's Game Boy, 2004's Nintendo DS, and 2011's Nintendo 3DS.

2. Sony Computer Entertainment: $7.20 billion

Even though it's just one part of Japanese mega electronics maker Sony, SCE takes second place among the biggest video game earners. SCE was founded in 1994 just before the release of the first PlayStation game console. So far, the company has released a new version just about every six years: PlayStation 2 in 2000, PlayStation 3 in 2007, and PlayStation 4 in 2013.

1. Microsoft Studios:
 ## $10.01 billion

This spinoff of Microsoft was founded as Microsoft Game Studios in 2002 just before it released the Xbox gaming system. In 2011 it was renamed simply Microsoft Studios. These days, the Washington State company produces games for the Xbox, Xbox 360, Xbox One *(below)*, Windows, and Windows Phones. As far as video games go, the studio's biggest sellers are those in its *Halo* series.

Feel like playing a video game, tracking your favorite basketball team, or checking in with a friend? Sometimes it seems as though *whatever* you want to do ... there's an app for that. In fact, there are millions of phone applications. But which ones have risen to the top of people's must-have lists? The answers are in the list below, which shows the 10 most downloaded apps and how many smartphone owners had used them as of July 2013.

10. Apple Maps: >>>> 19.3 percent of all smartphone owners

Ever since the iPhone *(right)* debuted in 2007, Apple has offered a Maps app to help you find your way, street by street and turn by turn. At first, Apple Maps was powered by Google Maps, but since 2012, it's used its own mapping information from non-Google sources.

9. Yahoo! Finance: 39.2 percent of all smartphone owners

Do the adults in your life put any of their money into the stock market? If so, chances are they want to see how their investments are doing. If a stock is doing well, it's time to celebrate. If it's on a downward slope, it's time to strategize. With the free Yahoo! Finance app, users can follow their stocks and get breaking financial news anytime, anywhere.

8. Pandora Radio: >>>>
40.4 percent of all smartphone owners

What's better than getting personalized music recommendations based on your favorite songs? How about an app that streams those songs right onto your phone? The brains behind Pandora consider more than 400 factors to match their music to their listeners. Users can download the app for free—and listen to ads—or pay for a subscription service that lets them skip the ads.

7. Apple App Suite:
43.9 percent of all smartphone owners

Not so much an app as a gateway to other apps, the Apple App Suite includes iTunes, Apple App Store, and Apple Game Center. So, if you're on an iPhone and you want to get music, apps, and games, you may as well download this app to get you started.

6. Gmail:
45.0 percent of all smartphone owners

Since 2004, millions of people have used Google's free Gmail service to send, store, and receive their e-mails. And since 2006, smartphone users have been able to download the Gmail app that lets them do it all on their phone: read, compose, reply, delete, mark as important . . . you get the picture.

5. Google Maps:
46.2 percent of all smartphone owners

This free app lets phone users access Google's top-ranked mapping service. Whether they're driving, walking, or riding the bus, travelers can rely on the voice-guided turn-by-turn navigation. They can also use the simple search for local restaurants, stores, and other attractions—and even see their friends' recommendations on the hottest spots.

4. Google Search:
53.5 percent of all smartphone owners

Wondering who won the Super Bowl last year, who sings that cool song you just heard, or what the capital of Zimbabwe is? You'll probably find your answers on the Internet. Google's search engine is the most used in the world—handling about 3 billion searches each day. Phone users get the same search power by downloading the free Google Search app.

3. Google Play:
53.6 percent of all smartphone owners

Does it ever seem as though Google really does rule the world? Coming in as the most popular of the four Google apps on this list, Play lets smartphone users access the full power of Google. From Google Play, users can browse and download any Google app, plus music, magazines, books, movies, and even TV shows.

2. YouTube:
53.7 percent of all smartphone owners

So maybe we lied about Google Play being the most popular Google app, since technically YouTube is owned by Google too. The YouTube app lets you keep up with your favorite videos, channels, and playlists anywhere your phone goes.

1. Facebook: 73.1 percent of all smartphone owners

It only makes sense that the world's most popular social networking site powers the most popular smartphone app, right? Nearly three-quarters of all smartphone users take advantage of a free Facebook download. They can keep up with friends and family while instantly sharing their thoughts, photos, videos, and more—all from the comfort of their phones.

A lot of technology is tiny. Computers, phones, and other devices seem to be getting smaller every day. But other kinds of technology take up more space. Take cars, for instance. Every motor vehicle runs on science and engineering wizardry. Of course, cars also run on actual fuel. One of the biggest recent developments in car technology has been the creation of more "green" vehicles that save fuel and cut down on harmful carbon dioxide emissions. And this tech is taking off. Here are the green cars that sold the most units (a.k.a. individual vehicles) in the year 2013*:

10. Chevrolet Malibu Eco with eAssist: 13,779 units

This "mild hybrid" runs on gas but is smart about getting the most for each gallon. The engine automatically shuts off when the car is coasting, braking, or stopped—and then restarts in a flash. A high-voltage battery in the trunk also helps boost the gas engine's efficiency. The model didn't return to dealerships in 2014 but may be back with fresh improvements in future seasons.

9. Toyota Avalon Hybrid: 16,468 units

Powered by a mix of gasoline and electricity, the Avalon Hybrid offers the best of both worlds. The team that makes it tick is made up of a gas-powered engine, an electric motor, and a battery to charge the motor. The Avalon just happens to be Toyota's largest sedan, but that doesn't stop this hybrid from eking out about 40 miles (64 kilometers) of every gallon in its gas tank.

8. Nissan Leaf: 22,610 units

The only 100 percent electric vehicle on this list first hit the streets in 2010. It runs on an electric motor powered by a built-in battery. That means no gasoline and no harmful carbon dioxide emissions. Like any other battery-powered device—think phones and MP3 players—the Leaf plugs into an electrical outlet to recharge. A full charge can power the car for up to 73 miles (117 km).

*Of vehicles with public sales numbers

A Chevrolet Volt boosts its battery at a charging station in New York City's Central Park.

7. Chevrolet Volt: 23,094 units

On an ordinary day, the Volt acts like an electric car. It can travel up to 38 miles (61 km) on a fully charged battery. Ready for a road trip? After that 38-mile mark, a gas generator kicks in to produce enough electricity for a longer journey. If travelers want to keep going after about 400 miles (644 km), they can just look for a power outlet, recharge the Volt, and keep on driving! A driver only has to stop at a gas station every 900 miles (1,448 km) or so.

6. Ford C-Max Hybrid: 28,056 units

The C-Max Hybrid had to work out a few glitches in 2013. When it turned out that the car had a lower-than-advertised mileage—about 40 miles (64 km) per gallon instead of the claimed 47 miles (76 km)—engineers got to work. They revamped the car's software control systems to boost electric-powered mileage, shorten the engine's warm-up time, and even make the air-conditioning system more efficient. Each upgrade reduced energy use and helped land the C-Max near the top of the sales heap.

^
^
^

5. Ford Fusion Hybrid: 37,270 units

Like its cousin, the C-Max, the Fusion Hybrid *(above)* got a technology makeover midway through 2013. It can travel 21 miles (34 km) on electric power alone—then log at least 600 more miles (965 km) on combined gas and electricity. At the end of the day, an owner can plug it in to charge overnight . . . or use a home charging station that gets the job done in just three hours.

4. Lexus hybrids: 43,582 units

The five Lexus hybrid models (RX, CT, ES, GS, and LS) on the market in 2013 pulled in enough combined sales to earn this spot on the list. Like many other hybrids, the Lexus cars boast efficient Atkinson cycle engines. First invented by engineer James Atkinson in 1882 (yes, that long ago!), it's the reason the Lexus Hybrid CT averages more than 40 miles (64 km) per gallon of gas.

3. Toyota Camry Hybrid: 44,448 units

What high-tech treats does this powerful sedan offer? Touch screen navigation? Check. Bluetooth connectivity? Check. Electric motor / gas engine combo? Check and check. And like most of its fellow hybrids, the Camry has another techy trick up its sleeve: regenerative braking. When the car slows down or stops, the electric motor captures the energy the car is losing and uses it to recharge the battery.

2. Volkswagen TDI: 95,823 units

Not all green vehicles use electricity to save fuel. The proof is in Volkswagen's four diesel-powered models (Jetta, Golf, Passat, and Toureg). Diesel, a liquid fuel, is more efficient than gas. For any of the Volkswagen diesel vehicles, a single gallon of diesel can last 30 to 40 miles (48 to 64 km). The TDI in these cars' names stands for turbocharged direct injection, the type of engine used—a fancy term for a fancy piece of technology.

1. Toyota Prius: 234,228 units

V
V
V
V
V
V
V

The Prius has come a long way since its 1997 debut. It's made its journey with an electric motor and a gasoline engine that can trade off or work together. The car itself automatically picks the most efficient power option at any given time, so drivers can sit back and enjoy the ride. They can also enjoy other techy perks. Exhibit A: solar panels on the roof power an interior fan that keeps the car cool when it's parked in the sun.

When you want the latest news, the best gossip, or just someone else's opinion, where do you turn? The Internet is technology's gift to the curious. It connects people across continents, time zones, and cultural divides. And it's stuffed with millions of online journals—a.k.a. weblogs, or blogs for short. To find out which ones stand out from the crowd, check out the most visited US-based blogs. We've ranked them according to their estimated number of monthly visitors as of December 2013.

10. TechCrunch: 8.5 million monthly visitors

Tech entrepreneur Michael Arrington launched TechCrunch from his California home in June 2005. Less than 18 months later, it had reached several million page views a month. This blog is by, for, and about techies. Whether you're looking for info on a new tech start-up company, the latest Internet products, or just breaking tech news, you can find it here.

9. PerezHilton: 12.7 million monthly visitors

Since first sharing his snarky take on celebrity behavior in 2004, Perez Hilton has become known as the Internet's most notorious gossip columnist. Specializing in rumors, juicy gossip, and unflattering paparazzi photos, his self-named blog is a must-read for celeb chasers and superfans.

8. *Daily Beast:* 13.5 million monthly visitors

Two media bigwigs—Tina Brown from the magazine world and Barry Diller from the TV world—launched the *Daily Beast* in 2008. Their idea was to help web surfers find the news they need and ignore the stuff they don't. The blog's popular Cheat Sheet column gives millions of viewers an always-changing list of links to news articles around the web.

7. Mashable: 14 million monthly visitors

This social media blog has been entertaining techies since 2005. Though its main focus is social media, it covers just about anything tech-related. A quick visit will turn up stories on cell phone behavior, entertainment, online video, business, web development, and just about any gadget you can imagine.

Many people check out blogs such as Lifehacker for advice on how to solve everyday problems at home or at school.

6. Gizmodo: 16.1 million monthly visitors

Dishing on gadget design since 2002, this tech blog has been translated into six languages other than English. Gizmodo is best known for an April 2010 stunt when the company bought a pre-release version of the iPhone 4 after someone accidentally left it in a public place. Gizmodo execs turned the phone over to California police, but they're still banned from all Apple events.

5. Lifehacker: 16.5 million monthly visitors

Its motto is "Tips, tricks, and downloads for getting things done." And that's pretty much what Lifehacker has been serving up on a daily basis since 2005. It takes its name from the term *life hack*, meaning "a simple solution to an everyday problem." As promised, it offers tips on technology, cooking, money, and many more aspects of everyday life.

4. Business Insider: 18.1 million monthly visitors

Since 2009, Business Insider has been providing the inside scoop on business and technology—and plenty of semi-related topics. Its site features original articles written by its staff of 50 as well as links to other info around the web. Got a burning question about how the latest tech company is doing? You'll find the answer here.

3. Gawker: 22 million monthly visitors

A focus on celebrity and media industry gossip keeps this blog's visitors coming back. With a pattern of highlighting people's mistakes and most embarrassing moments through leaked photos and e-mails, it has earned plenty of bad press and criticism. But it's also earned a solid following of media gawkers since its 2003 launch.

2. TMZ: 25 million monthly visitors

Looking for the latest paparazzi shot of your favorite celeb? You'll likely find it on TMZ. This L.A.-centered blog has been dishing out the latest dirt since 2005. It was the first to break a slew of stories about less-than-savory celebrity moments.

1. Huffington Post: 85 million monthly visitors

Towering above all the other blogs is the *Huffington Post*, with more than three times the monthly visitors of its closest competitor. How does *HuffPost* do it? For one thing, it covers everything from politics and business to entertainment and technology. It features both news and opinions, plus links to other articles across the web.

HIGHEST-PAYING COMPUTER TECH JOBS

Do you hope to someday have a career in the tech world? If you're a computer whiz, you may want to keep an eye on computer and information technology jobs. Plenty of these positions put workers at the cutting edge of tech—and some of them come with sizable paychecks too! These are the computer-related jobs with the highest average yearly salaries.

10. Database administrator: $77,100

Think about all the facts, numbers, and random information inside a computer. Database administrators make sure all that information is coded, categorized, and stored in the simplest way. They create, test, and make changes to computer databases with that goal in mind.

9. Computer systems analyst: $79,700

One reason these folks pull in the big bucks is that they work with entire systems instead of individual computers. They're always on the lookout for ways to solve problems and make computer systems faster and better. Think you'd like to try it? Head to school! Nearly half the nation's computer systems analysts have four-year college degrees and another 20 percent have master's degrees.

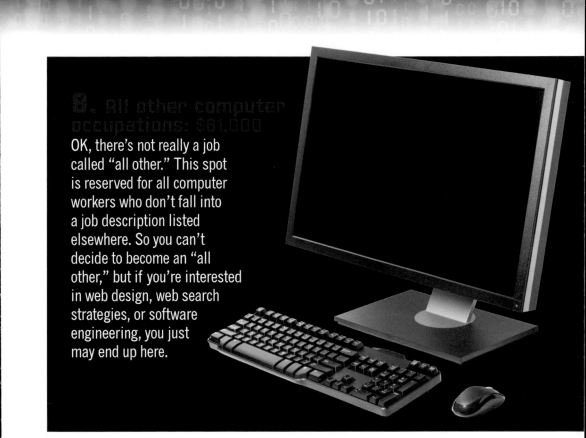

8. All other computer occupations: $61,000

OK, there's not really a job called "all other." This spot is reserved for all computer workers who don't fall into a job description listed elsewhere. So you can't decide to become an "all other," but if you're interested in web design, web search strategies, or software engineering, you just may end up here.

7. Information security analyst: $86,200

Think of these workers as the police detectives of the cyber world. They protect computers and computer networks from viruses, hackers, and other threats. Most of the job involves making sure the right protections are in place to safeguard computers and the personal information stored on them. Nearly two-thirds of these workers have a bachelor's degree or higher.

6. Software applications developer: $90,100

These are the techies who dream up, design, and build computer applications. They may work with designers, engineers, and other developers to make sure they create the most useful programs. Nearly half have four-year college degrees. Almost all have excellent critical thinking skills and a deep knowledge of computers.

5. Computer network architect: $91,000

If you know what intranet, extranet, LAN, or WAN is, this may be the career for you! Network architects do the same thing for computer networks that regular architects do for buildings. They design networks to make sure that all the complicated parts work together—and don't collapse on one another. The job calls for critical thinking and analyzing (and almost always, a college degree).

4. Software systems developer: $99,000

Unlike software application developers—who create, you guessed it, software applications!—these people work on entire computer systems. In a nutshell, they research, design, build, and test everything that happens in a computer system—for a hospital, a business, a school, or even the military. Interested? Concentrate your studies on computer science, engineering, and math.

<<<< ## 3. Computer hardware engineer: $100,900

If you think about hardware as the physical computer (rather than the instructions to the computer, which is software), then you get an idea of what hardware engineers do. They research, design, build, and test computers—along with any related equipment. If you want to get into this field, you'll first need to learn your way around computer gear such as circuit boards, processors, and computer chips.

2. Computer and information research scientist: $102,200

Research scientists are often the big thinkers behind the most complex computer systems. They're also the big guns who get called when developers run into serious problems. Computer technology in business, medicine, science, and many other fields depends on these experts.

1. Computer and information
↓ systems manager: $121,000

Systems managers need more than just great computer skills. They need to be good at managing people too. Someone in this position usually is in charge of all things computer-related at an organization. That means supervising lots of IT employees *and* working with others at the organization to meet their tech needs. People who nab these jobs often start out as developers, engineers, or systems architects. Nearly 70 percent have at least a four-year degree.

CONCLUSION

You've gotten a glimpse of the best of the best in the tech world. But technology is constantly changing. What's popular and profitable today might be old news tomorrow. A gadget you've never heard of might turn out to be the next big trend. To really stay in the loop, you'll have to keep your eye on the latest tech news. You just might stumble onto a whole new list of top tens!

You probably noticed that we used lots of different facts and figures to uncover the top 10 in each category. As you follow the shifting sands of technology, check for numbers, stats, or other ratings that can help you figure out what's at the top of the heap. Better get to work if you want to keep up!

Video chat is yet another form of technology you may use in your daily life. What criteria would you use to rank video chat services?

Now that you've checked out our top 10 lists, it's time to make your own! First, think critically about different kinds of technology. Come up with a list in a particular category that matters to you. Love space exploration? Your list may rank the most commonly used products developed by NASA. Obsessed with sending out Tweets to your followers? You might want to track the most influential people in the Twittersphere.

Make sure to determine and research your criteria for creating your list. For example, if you choose to list top video games, how will you determine which are the best? (Their sales figures? The length of time they've stuck around?) Add a few sentences about why you listed the people or things that you did.

Other Top 10 List Ideas

• Most expensive computers

• Most popular video games of all time

• Most common computer apps

• Oldest tech companies

• Smallest laptops

application: a computer program that performs a certain task

arcade game: a boxlike game played standing up in a public space, with each game paid for in coins

database: a collection of pieces of information that is stored and used on a computer

efficient: producing good results with little waste of energy, materials, money, and time

entrepreneur: someone who starts a business

founded: started

hardware: computer equipment

investment: putting money into something in the hope of gaining more money

IT: information technology, which involves the development and upkeep of computer systems, software, and networks

merger: when two companies join together to create one company

software: computer programs

stock: a portion of a company's value that can be bought, sold, or traded

video game console: the device that gives out the video signal to play a video game

Doeden, Matt. *Steve Jobs: Technology Innovator and Apple Genius.* Minneapolis: Lerner Publications, 2012.
Get to know the Apple computer founder, and learn more about the fascinating world of technology.

Donovan, Sandy. *Movies and TV Top Tens.* Minneapolis: Lerner Publications, 2015.
Check out more top 10 lists about your favorite TV shows and movies in this fun book.

Kids.getnetwise.org
http://kids.getnetwise.org
Get the best information on social media, safe Internet searching, and more at this site for kids and the adults who guide them.

Kids.gov: Online Safety
http://kids.usa.gov/teens-home/online-safety/index.shtml
This US government site for kids and teens offers tips and resources for online safety—plus links to more info on a whole bunch of tech careers.

Marsico, Katie. *Tremendous Technology Inventions.* Minneapolis: Lerner Publications, 2014.
Learn the strange stories behind technology inventions you use every day.

Woodford, Chris. *Cool Stuff 2.0: And How it Works.* New York: DK Publishing, 2010.
Wondering how all these amazing tech inventions actually work? This book explains the technology behind everyday objects such as cell phones, computers, and cars.

PHOTO ACKNOWLEDGMENTS

The images in this book are used with the permission of:
Backgrounds: © iStockphoto.com/kay (Binary code). © Granger
Wootz/Blend Images/CORBIS, pp. 4–5; © Jeff Greenberg/Alamy,
p. 6; AP Images for Nintendo America/Vince Bucci, p. 7; © Vince
Talotta/Toronto Star/Getty Images, p. 8; © Ina Fassbender/
Reuters/CORBIS, p. 9; © iStockphoto.com/macroworld, p. 10;
© iStockphoto.com/Pamela Moore, p. 11; © Robert Corse/iStock
Editorial/Thinkstock, p. 12; © Alex Segre/Alamy, p. 13;
© iStockphoto.com/teddyleung, p. 14; © Clarence Holmes/
agefotostock/SuperStock, p. 15; AP Photo/PRNewsFoto/Ford
Motor Company, p. 16; © Transtock/SuperStock, p. 17; © Clynt
Garnham Technology/Alamy, p. 18; © Scott Eells/Bloomberg via
Getty Images, p. 19; © iStockphoto.com/ LifesizeImages, p. 20;
© GaryPhoto/Thinkstock, p. 21; © John Fedele/Blend Images/
Alamy, p. 22; © Zoonar RF/Thinkstock, p. 23; © Maskot/Getty
Images, p. 24; © Fuse/Thinkstock, p. 25; © Robert Daly/OJO
Images/Getty Images, pp. 26–27.

Front cover: © iStockphoto.com/pictafolio, (joystick icon);
© iStockphoto.com/kay (Binary code).

Main body text set in News Gothic MT Std Condensed 12/14.
Typeface provided by Monotype Typography.